The *Birthday* Rose

What Katrina Could Not Destroy...

GWEN "MS. CHOCOLATE" WILLIAMS

The Birthday Rose
WHAT KATRINA COULD NOT DESTROY

Copyright © 2007
Reprinted: 2008

ISBN: 0-9747600-3-X (10-digit)
     978-0-9747600-3-2 (13-digit)

Printed in the United States of America
10 9 8 7 6 5 4 3 2 1

Cover Design, Text Preparation and Layout:
  Guardian Angel Communication Services
  Nashville, Tennessee
  gangelcs@comcast.net
  615.228.2688

Published by Gwen "Ms. Chocolate" Williams
Picayune, Mississippi

DEDICATION

This precious book is dedicated
to two of God's best roses:

Mrs. Mary Sims

and

Ms. Deseree Lucas

God has blessed my life with their
wisdom, love, prayers, advice, and laughter.

CONTENTS

INTRODUCTION

I COULD NOT BELIEVE another anniversary of the worst disaster in the history of America was fast approaching. I'd had a difficult time watching the replays during that first year because the wounds were so fresh. The scenes from my old neighborhood were still playing reruns in my brain. Hundreds of pictures in newspapers and images through the medium of television could never depict the unimaginable amount of rot and decay (that still exists throughout the city). There were no pictures to describe the deep, hidden feelings of the rich and famous or the poor and lonely.

Many homeowners who placed their trust in FEMA or the Road Home program are still waiting for money to rebuild their homes. Their lives are in the hands of crooked construction companies who make promises that will never come. With no money to rebuild, hope fades daily for many whose lives have come to a screeching halt. Those who were freely escorted "via slave planes and buses" to unknown promise lands pray daily that someone will provide a way for them to come home. Their promised lands are far better than the Ninth Ward of New Orleans, but its not home.

The labor force in New Orleans has been replaced by immigrant workers, many of whom made sacrifices to come to New Orleans to take advantage of the situation. Banks gave no thought to providing loans for their new business adventures. Soon, they had businesses on every corner and all the home folk could do was scratch their heads in wonder. Long lines of Hispanics wait at the construction sites and at the lumber companies hoping for a job. They have a reputation for being dependable and will work hard for the lowest price. Unfortunately, the home folk have no motivation or esteem to bargain with, so seem destined to remain on the road of poverty.

Every time I make that fifty-mile trip into the city from my comfortable nest in Picayune, I wonder if I am in the Twilight Zone. Many areas still resemble a war zone. I see the depression and stress on the faces I come in contact with. I listen to their stories of pain and frustration. Despite this sadness there is a splash of joy among those with an unshakable faith in Jesus Christ. Fortunately, I am one of those people.

There is still an ache in my heart whenever I go to visit the place I called home for over thirty years. Even though all of that time has passed, my missionary senses are as real today as they were when I took my first assignment at the homeless shelter. I am driven to go into the highways and byways to help make my brothers and sisters whole again. Yet I have no tears for myself. I have no storm story, but I have a story of God's faithfulness and deliverance. Katrina was a stepping stone to something greater that God was planning for me all along. I have always loved Romans 8:28, but Katrina shed new light on this precious verse.

Walk with me back to the beginning....

A ROSE IS BORN

I WAS NOT EXCITED about my fiftieth birthday. Even with my creative imagination, I had no clue about the meaning of being fifty. I knew none of the many experiences that folks my age talked about. I was never invited to such parties because the conversations were beyond my sheltered lifestyle. I accepted the fact that I had spent my entire life within the walls of the church. I'd never followed my peers to experience the ways of the world. If I had to backslide, it would be to a Sunday school class.

Despite being left out of the fast lane, I am thankful for my fantastic, boring life. I am thankful for all that God has done in my life and for the many places my tired feet have trod. I have fond memories of meeting many famous people and traveling to places that my parents had only seen in discarded magazines lying in the trash cans they emptied while they worked as a maid and a janitor. God has blessed me beyond words and I have no complaints about all that He has done for me. Although I have to admit sometimes I am jealous that my boring life does not move audiences or sell millions of books. Nevertheless, I have made an interesting discovery. I learned in seminary that God is omnipotent, meaning that He is all-powerful. Just as God has the power to rescue us from any pit, He also has the power to keep us from going there in the first place. I just decided that I wanted to be kept out of the pit and God has done His part.

Most of my peers celebrating their fiftieth birthday were married with grown children and grandchildren. They were living in their own house, either contemplating retirement or a second career. Meanwhile. I was single and still living in an apartment complex in New Orleans. I was trying desperately to get a ministry going, but getting nowhere. I wanted so much to write a New York Best Seller novel, but who would want to read about my boring life?

I was involved in lots of ministry activities, but had no money to show for my hard work. I was often laughed at for my commitment to missions. I tried writing for several publishing companies, but they often forgot to pay me. I was traveling home once a month to minister to the youth of my home church, but I felt unappreciated. I wanted so much for my church in New Orleans to get involved in missions, but the process dragged on year after year.

Furthermore, my dad had died the year before so without him there seemed to be nothing worth celebrating. I had spent most of the year fussing at God for allowing me to be left alone. I depended on my dad for everything. I worshipped the ground he walked. It was even worse for me that he'd died without remembering that I was his little girl. I could not understand why God did not heal my dad. He was such a great father, grandfather and husband. Questions, questions, and more question flooded my fifty-year-old brain as the Day of Doom approached.

As my birthday loomed closer, God sent a wonderful blessing by the name of Beth Moore. I had met her earlier and thought she was the greatest Bible teacher in America. The woman was real and had a love for the Word of God that many of us disciples only dreamed about. The day we met her first words to me were: "I want to come to your church." I was speechless. I heard that small voice declaring "This is the Lord's doing." My pastor, Dr. Fred Luter, gave the okay and we got started. Soon Beth Moore would be coming to Franklin Avenue Baptist Church in the heart of the Ninth Ward.

As plans for the Beth Moore conference came together I made an interesting discovery. I shared with unknown sisters and discovered a whole new family. The more we worked together God took all our experiences and wove them together into a tapestry of praise. I became the sugar in their lemonade and we all drank together from new wells of wisdom from God. The more we worked together the more I realized it was okay to have fun and be godly. God was taking me to a higher and different level—and one that I was ready for.

Beth taught us how to put our trust in GOD ALONE. I was a seminary grad, yet I had never heard of really letting God have everything. During my quiet time I realized that God could be Daddy, too. Hearing Him say He would spoil me better than my earthly father was a comforting relief. I could trust Him to take care of me and to provide me with whatever I needed. I never realized how true that promise would become.

In the midst of all this planning activity, I had no clue that my family and friends in Alexandria were doing some planning of their own. They managed to coordinate a big party in my honor. I had known nothing of the details of my big party, but had decided that I was going to have a great time. When I had gone to meet with the kids at the church that evening, I was surprised that Mom wanted to tag along. When we got to the church I was told to go wait in the sanctuary. The kids were all there, but they would not give a hint as to what was going on in the fellowship hall.

I wanted to know how they were and how they were getting along in school. They were quiet until the signal was given to bring me to the fellowship hall. I walked in and everybody yell a loud "Surprise!"

People were everywhere and so was the food. Starring at my wide brown eyes was the biggest chocolate cake I had ever seen. I missed my New Orleans family, but I was glad to see many old friends from my hometown. The older members who knew me as a youngster made their way to give me a hug. I am not the hugging kind, but this night was special. I received lots of presents from my kids, but Mom's gift had a really special meaning for me.

Mom was always good with her hands and could make the simplest gift look as if it cost thousands of dollars. I'd watched her make quilts, but never thought she would create a chocolate quilt for me. I was speechless as my eyes landed on the beautiful tan and brown quilt, loaded with replicas of the famous Hershey kiss. It was a masterpiece! Mom also presented me with a white vase holding one special rose. It was made by one of my dad's nurses at the hospital. I remember spending so many days there, hoping Dad would remember me. Mom noticed the nurse making roses from two-dollar bills and asked her to make me one. I liked my rose especially since it was made from money! At least now I would have the start of a nest egg for a rainy day.

A NEW MISSION

WHEN I RETURNED HOME to New Orleans my once-beautiful apartment had been transformed into a low income housing project. Kids were running around everywhere destroying everything in their path. They trampled the flower beds and played Tarzan with the branches of the trees. The new manager was no longer a resident at the complex so everybody had to fend for themselves. My fourteen years of comfortable living had come to an end. My new neighbors were the folks I ministered to in the ghetto, not folks I wanted to live with! It did not take the new children five minutes to discover that I was the candy lady. Before I could get settled, they were banging on my door wanting to know the price of the candy. They were surprised to find out the candy was free. It took a while for me to get the message that God had brought missions to my front door.

Each day brought more and more despair to my apartment complex. The new landlord refused to keep the place livable so I decided to be the advocate for the tenants. When I was not traveling telling stories I was on the phone fussing with whomever would listen to my complaints. I made the rounds to every agency that dealt with housing in New Orleans. Despite my best efforts, I did not get too many positive responses. I knew in my heart that God was not pleased and He would take care of business one of these days. Many nights I prayed that God would deal with all the evil and corruption in New Orleans.

My apartment complex became a haven for criminals and drug dealers. After blissfully living here for almost twenty years, it was now becoming a daily nightmare. In this entire situation God was always watching me as I tried to minister to the families. When I had to come home late at night the police would just happen to drive through the complex. I have to admit, though, that I was never really afraid of my new neighbors.

In the meantime, I was having a lot of problems with arthritis in my knees. Since I'd quit my job in 1994 to start my own ministry I no longer had health insurance. Each day the pain grew worse, but I had no money for the health care that I needed. Many days I found myself in line with my neighbors at a free clinic or charity hospital.

I was able to see for myself how bad the health care system was for the poor of New Orleans. I sat and waited long hours at the clinic to be examined by a wet-behind-the-ears resident who never learned my name. Everybody was so busy trying to make the rounds of the many people crowding the waiting room. I had always had good medical care, but many of these patients had no idea what good medical care was. They were given various drugs and told to come back later. There was no privacy or respect for these indigent patients. Listening to their conversations made me want to stand up and just scream. But I knew my pleas would only bounce against the dirty walls of the clinic.

Even though I was getting some medical attention, every day was a struggle to just get out of bed; but I never complained. The pain was so bad that I found myself watching those television faith healers hoping to hear them call out my ailment so I would be instantly healed. That day never came. I even enrolled in some clinical trials for arthritis treatments and that helped out for a while.

Meanwhile, God began to open opportunities for me to get inside the schools with stories about my life with my dad. I knew the first time I sat before the children that God was working on something special. I looked into searching faces wanting answers to problems education would never solve. I saw beautiful children created in the image of God to be great. I knew there had to be a way to get inside their brains with the message that they were the best thing on this earth.

On one occasion I was invited to a challenging school, and I had to admit that I was afraid. I knew I could not pray or share how Jesus could change their lives. I silently prayed, asking God for wisdom without getting thrown out of the school. I sat in that rocking chair and asked the children to repeat after me: "I'M GREAT! I'M SMART!" Then a voice from within said: "You want to learn an f-word?" I shocked myself, but I knew this had to be God. I instructed the kids to yell "I'M FANTASTIC!" They did it and that broke the ice. There was praise in my heart as I left the school.

That experience marked the beginning of my F-Word program. God was up to something and I was following His lead. I have to admit that some of the older kids were disappointed at my f-words. I knew the kind of f-words they heard at home or in their neighborhoods, but I was determined to change their attitude with positive f-words. I gave this to God with a prayer that He would show me how to get this message to all the schools.

God not only gave me a new mission, but he also gave my church a new vision for missions. I was working with the Woman's Missionary Union (WMU), but it was so hard to get them to see Christ beyond the doors of the church. I came to meetings fussing and fussing, but I got no attention.

Many youth groups came to work in New Orleans and they would always end up worshipping with us on Sunday morning. One morning I had had enough. I told my pastor that if he introduced another mission group I was going to stand up and scream like I had lost my mind. There were too many people in my church for us to sit and be entertained Sunday after Sunday. I knew God wanted to do something with my church and now was the time.

My prayers were answered in the spring of 1999 as my pastor commissioned Franklin Avenue Baptist Church's first mission group. My knees were killing me, but I was determined to go. I could not take the long van ride so I flew to South Carolina to meet the ladies. I wanted to cry as they were exposed to what I already knew. God was going to do something with this group and all I could do was raise my hands in praise.

These ladies were pioneers to teach many white missionaries that we were missionaries too. I watched those ladies work hard, teaching the children and even singing for the worship services. God was moving in such a miraculous way! They had their own mission stories and I knew my church would have to change.

 FRANKLIN AVENUE TO THE RESCUE

WHEN THOSE LADIES RETURNED to New Orleans there was a difference in their lives that everybody at church noticed. They could not stop talking about the mission trip. That confirmed for me that the youth of the church should form their own mission group. I gave the invitation for all interested youth to meet me in the chapel one day and, to my surprise, about fifteen of them showed up. When the pastor's son walked in I knew this group was going to be special. I had known Chip since he was two years old, but most of that time he had been the little brat that got on everybody's nerves. But I also knew Chip was a born leader and just what this group needed.

I worked hard with them and begged for money for their first mission trip. The youth pastor was just fantastic, traveling with us to make sure we had whatever we needed. The kids taught Vacation Bible School during the day and the youth pastor led revival services at night. The outreach minister went into the neighborhood to reach those who had no church home.

I told the kids that since this was our first mission trip we would keep it safe. They were to avoid the challenging areas in the neighborhood because I was afraid something bad might happen to them. I thought I would die when Chip returned saying he had witnessed to residents of a crack house. I did not know what to say, but thank God he came out alright!

When we returned to Franklin, I could feel the Spirit of God moving. God was preparing us for something greater, but I had no idea how God was going to make my church mission-minded. We had a great choir and fantastic preaching, but I knew God wanted more. God had gifted me with knowledge of missions, but I had no idea how to share it with my church. I loved to fuss, but no one paid attention to my fussing. Missions were just another social event.

Later the church decided to hire a new outreach minister and I just knew I was perfect for the job. Who knew more about missions than me? I was sure the pastor would think of no one else but me. Naturally, I felt rejected when someone else was chosen. But I refused to get upset; instead I prayed to God to show me ways to work with the new minister.

When we went on mission trips, the new minister of outreach was ready to travel with us. I planned a mission trip to Arkansas and the new minister, along with the minister of education, went with us. The kids worked in a food can salvage plant during the day and taught Vacation Bible School at night. God was moving in a miraculous way. The new minister of outreach became a great asset to missions at the church. I was glad to be of help to him. I also discovered that he was a great teacher and preacher.

Soon the mission fever made its way throughout the congregation. Several of the Sunday school classes were visiting nursing homes and homeless shelters. Several mission teams were organized to travel with other mission teams and to mission points within the state. I was proud of them as God taught them how to share the gospel. Most of those involved in missions were women so I decided that we needed to get the brothers involved.

I already had two of the men driving the bus so it was not hard to get others involved. I was able to gather about ten guys to do construction work. They were so excited they called themselves "Brothers on Mission." I started working on a mission trip for them.

Since the youth already had a relationship with a pastor in Dallas, I thought this would be the perfect initiation trip for the brothers. This pastor needed repairs on his church, but did not have the manpower for such a job. My mission bell went off and I decided that Brothers on Mission was ready to meet that challenge.

The men worked hard and soon eight of them were headed to Dallas to do repairs on this mission church. Since I don't cook, I got one of the ladies to travel with us to help with the food. Those brothers really worked hard and the pastor kept walking through the church with his hands in praise to God. I was never so proud of a bunch of men in my life! I was so excited that they even let me help paint the fence. (I just heard Brother Brooks laughing his head off.) The men were so inspired that they could not wait for the next mission project!

WMU at our church was growing and I could sense God preparing us for something, but I had no idea what. My prayer was that my church would become more mission minded. God had blessed us numerically and financially, but missions were always on the back burner. The potential was there, but we just needed a spark from On High.

My youth were growing and meeting challenge after challenge. Of course, the biggest challenge was losing the youth director to New York. The youth department was devastated and took a nose dive down the path of a "we ain't doing nothing" attitude. I had no idea what I could do to revive them. They missed the old director so much that they wanted nothing to do with the new preacher.

I tried hard to help, but most of the older youth I knew were already in college. This new bunch of youth was headstrong and only thought of themselves. I was determined to work with them, but I was reminded over and over how disrespectful they were. I was out of my league and I knew it. This new breed of youth was into having a good time, not serving like my older gang. As time passed, I could not get one of them to go on a mission trip.

There was another group of youth called the Circle of the Chosen that was different from the other youth ministries. Their director was really firm and demanding. I asked if she would mind if I took them on a mission trip. After much prayer and planning they were ready to go. They reminded me of my first mission team. They were very immature, but showed great possibilities. They finished the summer well and I was looking forward to what God was going to do in their lives.

Still, I questioned God over and over again as to what was I to do about missions at Franklin. We were too big and too talented to just sit and do nothing. Yes, I was proud of what we had done, but I knew God demanded more.

HURRICANE SCARES

NEW ORLEANS HAS ALWAYS BEEN an interesting city. Most tourists come for the food and Bourbon Street. Those of us who lived there knew that there was much more to New Orleans than tourism. New Orleans is surrounded by the mighty Mississippi River and Lake Pontchartrain. Even during a heavy rain, the water has no where to go.

During the months from June to November, we all know that a hurricane is possible. Every home is encouraged to get a hurricane preparedness kit, but most of the warnings are ignored. I was not born in New Orleans, so I sort of paid attention to some of the warnings. At the apartment complex, I lived on the second floor, but many days I watched the water rise in the complex parking lot.

I still have memories of what Hurricane Betsey had done to the city in 1965. I remember hearing the stories of how the rising water covered many of the homes in the lower Ninth Ward. I was in college at the time, but when I moved to New Orleans those stories became a warning. I was never afraid of the flooding because I lived in the eastern part of the city. I was always told that the east never flooded.

Even though I had lived in New Orleans several years, I don't ever remember being afraid during hurricane season. Since I was a missionary, my concern centered around my kids and the safety of their families. Whenever a hurricane warning was issued I always found myself staying so I could offer my help.

I remember when Hurricane Hugo was headed for New Orleans. It seemed like a pretty intense storm, but I made a decision not to leave. When church ended I went looking for a fellow missionary. I drove to her home and discovered that she had already left the city. I called my boss who suggested I go home to Alexandria with my parents. I decided that I would go home the following day.

During the night I woke up around three in the morning. I packed a small overnight bag, waiting for the news I dreaded. The news bulletin reported that the mayor suggested we evacuate the city. At the same time, my brother called and admonished me to leave right now. I got in my car and headed for the interstate.

It took nearly three hours to make the usual one-hour trip to Baton Rouge. I stopped at a truck stop to call my dad (who called me chicken) to inform him I was on the way. After driving another three hours, I was finally safe from the storm. Mom was glad to have me home safe and sound.

After the hurricane took a turn and decided to avoid New Orleans it was again safe to return. The city was safe and another hurricane season was nearly over. I did not mind the mini vacation to visit my parents, however. I was glad I had a safe place to go if another hurricane threatened us again.

When two of my senior adult friends moved to New Orleans, I became concerned about their welfare during hurricane season. When Hurricane Andrew made his way toward the city I immediately brought another senior friend to stay at my home. I knew she was afraid to be in her home alone. The hurricane avoided a direct hit, but its wind blew out the electricity. I had planned to spend the day in bed until the electricity returned, but my old friend wanted to get out of the house. We made our way to the Shoney's down the street that had power. Soon the power was on and everything was back to normal.

It became the norm every hurricane season to wait for the famous Nash Roberts to give the warning that a bad storm was coming. The city never prepared for a major evacuation, however; folks had a choice whether to leave or stay. Of course, many poor people had no means to leave so they had no choice but to remain for whatever. I had always jokingly said that God would not waste His wind to scare New Orleans—the city was just too corrupt to fear God.

I did not wait for Nash Robert's announcement when Hurricane Georges approached the Gulf of Mexico. I knew that my new landlord did not care about protecting us at the complex so I decided to head for home. I checked on my senior adult friends and discovered they had decided to stay. The mayor announced that the Superdome would be open for those who decided to stay. I packed a few things and headed for Alexandria.

I missed Dad being home to laugh at me for leaving, but I knew he was now with God. Mom was glad to have me at home. Of course the storm missed New Orleans, but it blew the power out. There was some flooding and wind damage in my neighborhood. After a couple of days I drove back to New Orleans. The three-hour return drive actually took five hours because so many people were returning.

When I arrived home my complex was a mess and the power still was not on. It was too hot to stay and my landlord refused to do anything for the residents. I asked one of my friends to store my food in her freezer since she had power. I jumped in my car and headed back to Alexandria. It was Mom's turn to have a good laugh.

I kept calling until I got the news that the power had been restored and it was safe to return. I was thankful that God

My brother James, Mom, and me.

had watched over New Orleans one more time. It wasn't long before crime and violence was back to normal in the Crescent City. It seemed that the more I prayed the worse it got. There was no safe place in the city. The FBI found one of the biggest drug lords in the country staying in my apartment complex. I remember one of the agents telling us that we could rest now. Who was he kidding? Through this entire ordeal, God was still good.

I continued to minister to the children at the schools and in my neighborhood. I ached inside that I had no message to reach them. They were only inspired by war stories that came from the police or wounded gang bangers. I spent many hours fussing and praying. It seemed like the gangs were winning and nobody could do anything to stop the violence. I prayed a daily prayer: "God, one of these days you are going to wipe New Orleans out. Just give me a warning so I can grab my purse and get out!" I was serious, but not thinking God was listening. Every year more murders were committed and I kept praying my routine prayer. I had a feeling...

I was watching television when the announcement came that another hurricane was headed for Louisiana. We had gone through this ritual so many times before that I had delayed leaving. Forgetting the words of my daily prayer I grabbed my standard overnight bag and headed for Alexandria. I called my brother on the cell phone and joked about how slow the traffic was moving. I made myself comfortable as the traffic inched along. I was still ahead of most of the traffic.

I was safe and sound in Alexandria while others headed out of New Orleans were stuck in traffic for over fifteen hours. I learned that the mayor had called for an evacuation, especially in the low areas of New Orleans. I believe folks were really scared this time. I heard stories traffic being so heavy that it took some people ten hours to drive as few as twenty-five miles. I did not have the patience to stay in regular traffic so I was thankful that I had left early. The stories of what went on in the Superdome and some of the relief centers while people waited out the hurricane were just as alarming. I thought to myself: "What is the world coming to?" Like so many others, that hurricane missed

New Orleans and hit somewhere else. In about a week things were back to normal again.

Probably because of all of these false warnings, the hurricane season of 2004 was a warning that nobody heeded. One of the university professors gave a report that if New Orleans was ever hit by a major hurricane there would be massive flooding because the levees would breach. I paid no attention to his prediction and apparently neither did anybody else. I guess somebody gave money for a hurricane study and this professor was just giving his report. Between the professor's report and my daily prayer none of us were paying attention.

# GOD'S WARNING

AS IF ENDURING SEASON after season of hurricane warnings had not been bad enough, things had gotten so bad at my apartment complex that I could not take another day there. I loved ministering to the people, but the landlord cared nothing about the residents. The more I complained the more he ignored needed repairs around the complex. Every day was a constant battle that seemed I would never win.

But the Lord was still with me in so many ways that I could see. God provided a way for me to get my knees replaced at a hospital in Jackson, Mississippi. This was a blessing, but I missed being away from my kids so long. It would take a couple of years of surgery and physical therapy before I would be able to walk without pain. I was away from the complex during this time, but when I returned I was ready to give my landlord the fight of his life. I knew Satan was a tough foe, but I also knew that the battle was God's, not mine.

One evening I was watching television and discovered a bumble bee buzzing in my afro. I could not imagine bees in my apartment flying at this time of night. I swung and missed the bee, and he stung me anyway. Where did he come from? Before I could get over the shock of that bee, another one was buzzing around the ceiling fan. This was going to be fun, so I thought.

The next day I heard another bee buzzing behind the curtain in my bedroom. When I pulled the curtains back I had the shock of my life. There were several bees buzzing in harmony looking for a way outside. I grabbed my fly swatter and swung away. Before long I had about twenty bees headed for bee heaven. I noticed several holes in the screens on the windows. Since I was on the second floor, I figured that the bees must have built a hive near the roof. I decided to complain to the manager with the hope of getting the screens replaced, but I was wrong.

I already knew that the manager cared nothing about me so the bees were just another item on her list. Every evening I was swatting bees inside my apartment. It was not unusual to find one on the wall wishing me good night. I had decided to sleep in the extra bedroom until I discovered there were as many bees inside that window. I still had no idea how the bees were getting inside my apartment.

I went to the store to purchase bee killer. The pest agent informed me that I could not kill the bees; I had to call a bee exterminator. I ignored the agent and purchased a can of wasp/hornet killer and decided to get rid of those bees. The can of spray would shoot about twenty feet so I was ready.

I was shocked when I discovered a hole beneath the roof where the bees were swarming. Apparently they were building a hive inside that hole that led to the attic. I aimed that spray and the bees took off inside their hidden home. I guess I made them mad because when I got inside there were hundreds inside the screen on my window. I called the manager and she was going to call a bee keeper the next day. The next day never came and I kept fighting and fighting bees. I decided to take matters into my own hands.

I picked up the phone and called every television station in New Orleans. I called the housing authority and the health department to complain, but no one paid any attention to my dilemma. Finally one of the television stations called my landlord who informed them he would take care of the bees. He did nothing. An inspector came by and I showed him my plastic bag filled with dead bees. He shook his head and said he was going to turn my landlord in. Of course, nothing happened and I was still fighting with the bees.

One Sunday morning I was trying to get dressed for church when I heard that buzzing from the window. I threw back the curtain and discovered thousands of bees inside my window. They were everywhere. I panicked at the thought of them making their way inside the room. I hurriedly dressed and headed for church. I tried to hear a word from God, but all I could think about was those bees all over my apartment when I returned home.

I called the manager and begged her to do something about the bees. She refused to return my calls so the next day I called the television station again. They got in touch with the landlord who sent the manager to see for herself my collection of bees. By the time she arrived I was praying one of the creatures would give her a taste of his stinger! She apologized and promised to send someone over to get rid of the bees.

The next day I discovered a dude on a ladder outside my window. He had a water hose to scare away the bees. He also had a bucket of something that he used to plug up the hole where the bees were entering the attic. I had a fit, but I did not know what to do. After he plugged up the hole I knew the bees would find a way to get inside to their newly-built hive. I could hear their buzzing inside my walls. I tried to put a little humor in the situation by hoping I could at least get a jar of honey out of the deal.

As if the bees weren't enough, the apartment complex became a haven for every crook and drug dealer in New Orleans. There was no on-site management at the complex so it was every man for himself. There were a couple of older tenants that I knew, but most of the new residents were survivors of welfare and Section 8. They were just glad to have a roof over their heads so they did little complaining.

One afternoon I heard such a commotion outside that I was ready to run for cover. One of my neighbors knocked on my door urging me to come and see. I opened my door to several FBI agents hauling away a guy in handcuffs. One of the agents yelled that we were safe now. This guy was a wanted drug dealer and he was hiding in the complex with over $40,000.00 in cash and lots of drugs! My heart ached for the children who stood silently watching. I walked back inside my safety zone shaking my head like Habakkuk: "Lord how long?" I found my familiar prayer spot in my recliner, praying: "God, one of these days you're going to wipe out New Orleans. All I ask is that you give me a warning so I can grab my purse and get out of here."

Every day the news was the same—filled with drug-related murders, drive-by shootings, domestic violence, and, to ice the already foul-smelling cake, corruption. New Orleans was the epitome of the phrase "I don't care and show me the money." Politicians could no longer be trusted and many of them were making daily confessions of wrong-doings. The school system had become a haven for violence and drug-dealing rather than a place of learning. Good teachers were forced or driven to retirement and those remaining were too fresh to deal with the many problems facing them daily. Teachers had the added roles of police, nurse, parent, social worker, counselor, and preacher. I was thankful that I was still invited to share my stories with the children. Teaching them to yell that they were fantastic was not working like I wanted it to. There had to be way to show them that they were valuable and created to be great without mentioning God. I prayed for God to show me a way to reach these children before the world dragged them farther into the pits of poverty and despair.

As the crime in New Orleans increased so did the number of mega churches. There was a church on every corner it seemed, practicing whatever was popular. Tourists made their way to the most popular churches to rock out with the choir and jam with the preacher. You name it and it was preached and practiced in every church in New Orleans. Preachers covered the airwaves boasting of their latest book, CD, and an invitation to their latest show-and-tell conference. These places where God intended His gospel preached and followed had become places of business and entertainment.

The church was a place of comfortable, complacent folk who came to tip God and add to their social calendar.

Fortunately, Franklin Avenue Baptist Church was not like that. I was thankful for a pastor who continued to preach the gospel every Sunday. My church had grown to nearly seven thousand members who came because of Christ. The problem with my church was what I called "spiritual constipation." They packed God's house and sat at His table to feast and feast, but never produced anything. They were spiritual gluttons who refused to share what they learned with anybody. They filled the pews until we had to put chairs down the isles and extended the services from one to three each Sunday. We looked like a bunch of Humpty Dumptys sitting on a spiritual wall, waiting for God to drag us over the Pearly Gates.

I was shocked when the church asked me to speak for woman's day in 2004. The theme was: "Going for the Gold," and I yielded myself to God's spirit as I prepared for the service. As I walked into the sanctuary I sensed an unusual spirit in this familiar place. When it was my turn to speak something got a hold on me that I could not explain. I looked into familiar faces declaring: "Franklin Avenue, you are sitting in a gold mine but you don't know it." Waving my hand at all that God had blessed us with, I further stated: "You see all of this? You can lose it." I had no

I spoke a word of warning at Franklin Avenue's women's day program. The theme was "Going for the Gold."

idea that this was a warning from God. The service ended with lots of praise to God, but no attention to His words.

God was trying to prepare my church, but none of us were listening. My pastor had decided to call a forty-day fast at the beginning of 2004. We were to use the *Purpose Driven Life* by Rick Warren as our guide for the fast. I could see something stirring within our congregation, but I had no idea what was going on. People began to confess their complacency, but they seemed afraid to do anything about it. The last chapter in Warren's book dealt with missions, so my pastor asked me to team teach with him. I jumped at the chance to expose my church to a world that needed what they already knew. I taught from my heart and got a good response from the church. The last night of the teaching I was so blessed, but Satan was waiting for me when I returned home.

When I got home, I found that my apartment had been ransacked by one of the tenants. They were drug dealers searching for money or something to sell to purchase drugs. They were too lazy to unplug my old computer so they left it in the middle of the floor. They turned my mattresses over thinking I had hidden money there, but missed the bank bag sitting in the middle of the bed! All they got away with was a cheap ring and my chocolate valentine candy. I was more hurt than ever to think that the very people I risked my life to help would try to rob me. I just praised God for His protection. I found my way to my prayer spot, still questioning God: "HOW LONG?"

I could not take my apartment complex any longer. Every day I was fighting bees and trying to live despite my fear of another break-in. I prayed for another place to live. I went to house-buying class, but I never had enough income to purchase a home. My good friend Beth Moore came out with another book teaching us how to believe God. At first I thought Sister Girl had lost her mind! The more I read her book the more I submitted to the fact that I believed in God, but I did not believe God. I decided to give it a try. In her study course on Believing God, she encouraged us to wear a blue string to remind us to practice and say five truths about God and His Word. There were several realtors in my church so I asked one of them to find me a house.

I pulled on my blue string as I met with the bank loan officer at my bank of more than twenty years. The lady was nice, but she said the bank could not loan me money to purchase a home. I was disappointed but still believing God for my new home.

My realtor knew of another house buying class that could help me. The director of the program added to my blue string as she encouraged me to seek a grant from the city to help with the purchase. I had no idea what she was talking about, but I believed God. I attended all the classes and soon I was sitting with a loan officer from another bank. I was shocked that these unknown folk were willing to assist me, along with the grant from the city, to purchase a house.

Because I had little income my realtor had few choices to offer for a house. I told God I wanted a brick, three-bedroom, two-toilet, air-conditioned house in a safe neighborhood. I was not excited when my realtor showed me a tiny wood-framed house in the Ninth Ward, located right next to the Jewel Box Lounge. This was not an answer to my prayers— or was it? God was up to something, but I had no clue. I decided to try and buy this house that I had already called "my little Shacky Shack." I just wanted to get out of that complex at any cost.

I was told that it would take months to get approval for the grant from the city so I was preparing for the long wait. Nevertheless, the inspector came during the last of November and the grant was approved the next week. When I went to pick up my papers the clerk could not understand how the paperwork had been processed so quickly. I pulled on my blue string and shared my faith promise with her. I think she thought I was joking, but I shared anyway. When I showed my papers to the bank officer she could not believe it either. I just knew God was up to something and before I knew it I was packing to move.

I stood on the familiar balcony of my apartment complex and tried to explain to the children that I was moving. I held my candy basket for the last time trying to fight back tears. I was headed for something better, but I hated leaving the children. They looked at me with their sad eyes wondering who would give them candy. Who would check their report cards? Who would give them school supplies? I gave them a hug and told them that I would continue to come by with candy and school supplies.

Several of the men from my church along with my mom helped me move into my new home. There were many senior adults on Piety Street and I soon discovered that the Jewel Box was a night club for old folks. It was open only on the weekend and the patrons were always nice to leave me a parking space on the street. Aside from the loud noise I felt pretty safe in this neighborhood. I was less than a mile from my church and my neighbors looked out for me when I came home late at night. This was not what I had wanted, but rather what God wanted for me. My mortgage notes were so low that I figured I could pay for this house in ten years. But I could hear God telling me He could pay my mortgage off in less than three years. That was a tall order, but I gave my blue cord a yank and believed God.

I wished myself a Happy New Year as 2005 revealed itself to the world. I was content to be in my new home and I was excited to play homemaker. I loved my new prayer spot where I could listen to God and pray for all my children. This was not my dream house, but it was certainly a step up from my old apartment complex. I missed my kids, but I was looking forward to meeting the kids in this neighborhood. One of my grown-up kids decided I needed a dog so she brought "Silky" to share my Shacky Shack. Mom and my sister-in-law Rie came to plant flowers in the front yard. Along with the music from my wind chime and the music from the nightclub down the street, I would say I loved my new place. This was not the house I had prayed for, and somewhere inside my spirit I knew I would not be here long.

Since I lived so close to the church I practically lived there. Pastor had decided to lead us in reading through the entire Bible that year. I was asked to teach a class for the woman's ministry and for Sunday school. Things were going so well that the church voted to purchase several acres of land in New Orleans east. Our church needed more land, especially for parking. The night we voted I sort of had mixed feelings about the move. My mind recalled the story of the rich man with the great harvest. Instead of finding a way to share his crop, he instead chose to build a bigger barn. He died leaving his harvest and the big barn. What was God trying to say? There was an uneasy feeling I could not shake. I kept my feelings to myself, but I knew God was about to take my church and me on a different journey.

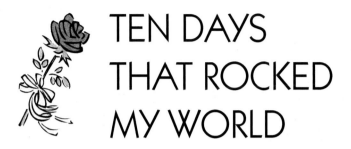

TEN DAYS THAT ROCKED MY WORLD

THE SUMMER OF 2005 was filled with my getting used to being a homeowner. It was more expensive than renting an apartment, but at least this place was mine. I had to get used to fixing things myself, but at least I knew it would get fixed. I was so excited to have my own hammer, rake and ladder. My flowers were so pretty and I had the prettiest yard on the block. I had fun chasing Silky around the yard and watching him bark at the children passing by. I was hoping to get to know them so I could spoil them with chocolate.

I was still discovering my new house and praising God for His blessings. The house was small and I had to put some boxes in the attic because I had little storage space. All in all, I was just happy that I was in a safe place with no bumble bees!

Missions at Franklin were going so-so, but I was just trying to be patient and watch God move. God was moving among the men as they decided to do a home makeover for one of the senior citizens in our church. Pastor led the way and the men followed. Of course, I was in charge of the project. Since I was a new homeowner I figured the knowledge would do me some good. The Johnson's house was in bad shape, but the Brothers on Mission wanted to give it a try. The brothers could only work on the weekends, but they promised to have it finished before winter. The men came together and cleaned the property and gutted out the house. This was a new project for them, but I was sure they could handle it.

While the men were working on the house, during the summer I took the youth on two mission trips. It was hard getting a committed group, but I managed to draft fifteen of them. The first trip to Tennessee was very challenging, but rewarding. I had a feeling that God was preparing us for something big. I watched my older kids tackle some hard situations as strong believers. All my years of fussing were finally paying off. I had no idea they were about to face the biggest challenge of their lives.

The second mission trip was to my dad's hometown of Bunkie, Louisiana. The First Baptist Church there had started a small mission church in the black section of town. A youthful, inexperienced minister had been chosen to lead the small flock. There was a small, well-kept housing project next door to the church so my kids conducted a challenging Vacation Bible School. I brought in one of the younger ministers from Franklin to lead the revival each night. My brother even came to play the drums. I have to say we made some Holy Ghost noise in that neighborhood! When the week ended I promised the young minister that we would be back the next summer.

Summer was nearing an end and so far no hurricane had touched our shores. While the men were still busy working on the Johnson home, I decided to have some fun at camp. While at camp I finished up some writing assignments, spent some time with Mom, and found the biggest watermelon in Sugertown, Louisiana. I had one more speaking engagement then I could rest for a while.

I decided to start an exercise program at a nearby hospital to work off more weight. I was so proud that I already had lost over fifty pounds and my doctor was really pleased. I returned Silky to my youth who had given him to me, who gave him to a relative in Tennessee. I sure missed him, but the day soon would come when I would be glad he was gone. I guess I was footloose and fancy free. I bought an air conditioner so I could relax in the evenings. As August came to an end, I settled for a little R&R. Then it happened....

DAY ONE: Friday, August 26, 2005

It was so hot that day, but I decided to make it to exercise class anyway. I really had a good workout that day. I made it back to my little Shacky Shack just in time to hear the noonday news. The weather man said a hurricane was brewing in the Gulf and it had the potential of being a very strong storm. I had heard that same story so many times before that I was not alarmed. I was concerned about the men working on the Johnson house, however. I called to check on things and they informed me that the plumbing and electrical work were completed. Yeah!!!! Brother Gettridge informed me that he would go over on Saturday morning to finish up a few things and that the sheet rocking would begin on Monday. That was exciting.

The singles had asked me to speak at their retreat at our east campus. The news of the approaching hurricane seemed to fall on deaf ears. I got dressed and headed for the campus. When I arrived I just happen to see the ducks in the pond by the chapel. I grabbed my camera and clicked away. I went inside and the singles were waiting. I sensed something different going on, but I could not put my finger on it. They had plenty of food and I really enjoyed the fellowship.

It was after ten o'clock when I got home so I missed the evening news. I was tired so I went to bed early.

• • • • • •

DAY TWO: Saturday, August 27, 2005

I was awakened at 6:00 a.m. by a phone call from Mom. She wanted to know if I was on my way. I was so sleepy, but I told her I would probably come home after Sunday services. That was the usual protocol whenever a hurricane was approaching. Mom said she would leave the gate opened for me. I told her that the latest news on Hurricane Katrina was that if she did not turn around noon; the mayor would request an evacuation of the city. I told her again that I would wait and come home after services on Sunday. I hung up the phone and went back to sleep.

For some reason I just tossed and turned until almost eight. I saw the tracking map of Katrina and it looked like she was headed straight for New Orleans. I got up and decided to start checking on folks. I called one of my senior friends and she said she was leaving right away. I put on my same clothes that I had worn to the retreat and put my dirty clothes in a laundry bag. I thought since I would be away only for a couple of days I didn't need many clothes. I always kept a change of clothes at mom's house. I was headed out the door and something said *"Get your laptop computer."* That was strange because I had no intention of doing any work. Something also told me to get the disk that carried the thoughts of my million dollar novel. I picked up the disk and the computer and headed for the trunk of my car. I didn't even think about my computer case, I just dumped everything in the trunk.

It was almost eleven by then, so I drove to visit my two senior sisters to check on them. When I got to their home one of the sisters was in frenzy and the other sister decided to make her home in the bathtub until the hurricane was over. I told them I was headed for Alexandria and they could both come with me. While I was there one of the sons called to check on his mom, but I still could not convince them to go home with me. They did promise that if things got really bad they would go to the Superdome. I did not like that idea at all, but I knew I was fighting a losing battle. I wished them well and headed back home.

On the way home I stopped to check on Brother Gettridge, who was still working on the Johnson house. He showed me all the work the men had completed and I was so excited. This old couple would finally have a decent place to live. Brother Gettridge had no lunch so I told him that I would run to a nearby fast food place and bring him back something to eat. I listened to the news on the way to the fast food place and people were getting on the highway in record numbers. I brought the food back to Brother Gettridge and headed for my house. I stopped at a red light on Franklin Avenue and I heard a voice saying *"Don't go back to the house. Get on the highway."* I obeyed the voice and headed for I-10, but not toward Metairie. I found myself headed toward Slidell. I did not panic, but followed the advice of the voice ringing in my head.

There was not much traffic on the way to Slidell, but I met the multitude when I turned onto the interstate that led to Baton Rouge. It had taken nearly two hours to drive the thirty miles, but I was still calm. It was almost 3:00 p.m.

when I heard on the radio that the mayor would start the contra-flow at 4:00 p.m. Then I got scared. I feared that I would be forced to go to Jackson or Natchez, Mississippi and I did not know how to get to Alexandria from either of those places. I tried to call by brother James on my cell phone, but I could not get him. I called Mom and told her I was on the way. She was relieved, but at that moment I had no idea how long it would take for me to get home.

I made it to Baton Rouge before the major traffic jam so it was smooth sailing the rest of the journey to Alexandria. It was almost seven o'clock that night before I got home, but Mom was glad I was away from New Orleans. I brought in my few pieces of dirty laundry and I told Mom I could wash them on Monday. I settled down in front of the television to catch the latest on Hurricane Katrina. The hurricane did not turn as was hoped; she was headed straight for New Orleans.

James came over that evening and said he had been tracking the storm on the Internet. I figured it would be bad, but never imagined the sort disaster that was brewing. I watched the news until I fell asleep on the sofa.

• • • • • •

DAY THREE: Sunday, August 28, 2005

I woke up early to listen to my favorite preachers on the television, but my thoughts were on the storm. Before I could wipe the sleep out of my eyes I knew the news was bad. I grabbed the phone and started calling. I called my two elderly sisters and discovered that they were on their way out of town. I urged them to keep their cell phone on and I would check with them later. I called my pastor and Liz and they were already in Birmingham with their daughter. I got the phone numbers of some of my other friends so I could check on them. I had no phone or address book with me. I called my good friend Deseree and she was on her way to Houston. Things were getting serious and it looked bad for New Orleans.

None of us went to church that Sunday. We stayed by the television and listened to news of the approaching storm. The grim news brought stillness all through the house. My mom kept quiet and Boris, Mom's favorite dog, had no idea what was going on. We watched in awe as the slow-moving lanes of traffic headed away from the city. Periodically, the newscasters showed the crowd that had gathered at the Superdome.

I was glad to be home with Mom, but I was concerned for my church family and friends I had left behind. I did not take my computer out of the trunk because I knew that I would be headed back as soon as the storm was over. By evening, the storm was listed as a category four, and that was really bad. Katrina packed the same kind of powerful winds as the never-forgotten Hurricane Betsy. I remembered how bad the flooding was then, but had no idea we were headed for a repeat performance.

• • • • • •

DAY FOUR: Monday, August 29, 2005

I was awakened that morning by the phone ringing. It was James wanting to know if I was watching the news. I had tossed and turned on the sofa all night, so I had no idea what was going on. I think my mind was still in New Orleans. Boris decided he wanted to go outside so I had to get up. When I turned on the television, there was still Katrina headed straight for New Orleans and folks were still waiting for the worst. Katrina was packing winds over 150 miles per hour, which made her the most dangerous storm ever to hit the city.

My eyes were glued to the television screen as the news reported every mile the storm was closer to the city. I watched in horror as the howling winds blew out the windows of the famous Hyatt Regency hotel located next to the Superdome. I saw roofs flying and trees swaying to the beat of no Mardi Gras parade. The winds were so fierce that it blew the roof off the Superdome. The people panicked in the darkness with nowhere to run for cover.

Just as the storm was to hit New Orleans directly, it turned eastward and headed for the Mississippi Gulf Coast. I breathed a sigh of relief and told Mom that I would probably return home tomorrow. Those words were short lived as the next breaking news reported the breaching of the levees in New Orleans. I had no idea what the reporters were talking about. I knew what breach meant, but I did not know those levees were holding back that much water. My next sight was water, water, and more water. I had never seen so much water in all my life. In a matter of hours 80 percent of the city was under water.

Since my house was already three feet off the ground, I assumed that everything was alright in my neighborhood. The lower Ninth Ward and St. Bernard Parish had taken most of the water. I breathed another sigh of relief, thanking God that my area was probably safe from the water. I could not imagine my house or my church being included in the flooded 80 percent of the city. My mouth fell wide open as the cameras revealed the devastating verdict. This was no late-night movie; this was really happening. I held on to a pillow, trying to face the music of a sad song I did not want to hear. Ray Nagin, the mayor of New Orleans, added to the grim news announcing the lost of homes and life.

The Red Cross and the Corp of Engineers had men and helicopters searching for those who were caught in the flood or stranded on rooftops. I was too shocked to cry. I knew there was nothing I could do. Mom and James had no idea what they could say to bring a sense of comfort to my disbelieving look. I could see people being lifted from the waters and hauled to the already overcrowded Superdome. And the water was still rising. Since there was no electricity, no water, and no air conditioning, droves of people sat miserably waiting for someone to tell them what to do next. Many of them were elderly or had other medical needs.

Again I watched television until I fell asleep on the sofa. As I drifted off, my thoughts continued to bounce on and off between belief and unbelief. I kept thinking that I would awaken and discover that I had been in the Twilight Zone. I kept expecting the announcer to say "We will now join our regularly scheduled television program." That announcement never came. The picture was still as grim as it had been on yesterday.

• • • • • •

DAY FIVE: Tuesday, August 30, 2005

My eyes awakened to the cries of hundreds of people needing help. I could not imagine the vast multitude of people who were stranded in the city. The television revealed people wading in water that came up to their heads. Cries came from those trapped in attics with no way to get out. With no water or power inside, those stranded at the Superdome waited out front for buses that never came. Government officials came and made useless promises. FEMA made promises they would never keep and the crowds swelled to several thousand trying to survive the worst disaster in American history.

My eyes panned the crowd, searching for a familiar face, but there were too many faces to jog my memory. The crying children found a familiar spot in my heart, but what could I do? I gasped when I saw folks looting stores with anything they could carry. I could understand taking water or food, but seeing the youth running with a television was beyond my comprehension. The police had their hands full, but this was a battle they would never win. Folks who had been rescued by boats or helicopters were dropped off at the Superdome, adding to the swelling masses gathered outside the doomed mega structure. Meanwhile, the people raided any building downtown that had water or food. I could not believe this was not a movie or documentary program; this was really happening.

I was thankful to be safe and secure at Mom's, but my heart was buried among the crying and dying in New Orleans. I silently prayed for the unbelievable situation in New Orleans and that God would send a Moses to rescue them. I opened my eyes to look into the eyes of a troubled little dog who had his paw on my lap. Looking into Boris's sad little face I could almost hear him say, "Everything is going to be alright." My brains were so scrambled that I did not know what to do. I knew that it would be weeks before I could go home and I had no medication or clothes. I ran to my car to retrieve my computer. Mom was never into technology so I had no idea how I could hook my computer to her antique phone system.

I remembered that I had left a modem plugged in the phone jack from my last visit. I hooked everything up and soon I was online. My laptop was so old it took forever to do anything on it, but at least I could communicate. I could not remember any of my passwords, so it was like starting all over again. AOL was so helpful with helping me retrieve messages from so many friends who wondered where I was. Every time I got an e-mail it was like getting a warm cup of hot chocolate.

Mom rode with me to Wal-mart to get refills on my medications. I will always thank those folks for their kindness during such a difficult time. While waiting for my medicine, I realized that I had nothing, absolutely nothing. I stared at an eyebrow pencil and broke out in a cold sweat. Mom got me to a seat in the pharmacy department. She kept saying something, but I just could not comprehend what she was saying. For a moment I believed I was in the Twilight Zone. I think I told her I would be fine just let me sit for a minute. For the first time I realized I had lost everything I owned.

Since it was the end of the month I had no money so Mom had to pay for my medicine. She asked what else I needed and I was just too numb to even think of an answer. I just wanted to get somewhere quiet to process everything.

• • • • •

DAY SIX: Wednesday. August 31, 2005

Sometime during the night God showed up and gave me much needed rest. I awoke a familiar voice that I use to hear in my comfortable place in my Shacky Shack. "I am here too. I have a plan. Just be still and wait." This was my assurance that God was up to something and I would be alright. I prayed for wisdom to understand the process of being displaced. I got my computer running and found the Web site with all the information I needed. I managed to get my address changed and apply for the many services made available to persons displaced by Katrina. I still needed all my important papers, which I imagined were floating somewhere in the Ninth Ward of New Orleans.

Every time worry approached my mind, I had this familiar feeling that everything was working out for my good. The television painted more grim pictures of the suffering and devastation of a city under water. I saw Mayor Nagin almost in tears trying to do what he was never elected to do. I remembered the many times he had come to worship at our church and I prayed that some of what he'd heard there would comfort him during this difficult time. There was water everywhere, but there was none to drink for the thousands stranded in the Superdome and the convention center.

Mom joined me watching the rescue and recovery operation of the National Guard and the Red Cross. Once and a while the cameras panned my neighborhood and all I saw were roof tops and floating debris. People were screaming for help or crying because of the loved ones they'd had to leave behind. It was not a pretty sight. The police were running around, hoping to catch the looters who were trying to make a fast getaway to nowhere.

My Palm Pilot needed to charge before I could retrieve phone numbers, but I realized that my cord was floating somewhere in my flooded house. I would not get discouraged, however, because I had something inside telling me everything was going to be alright. I spent most of the day trying to connect to the Internet. It took a while, but soon I was getting e-mails from friends.

I had none of my tapes, but my mind recalled the words to a favorite song from the Brooklyn Tabernacle Choir:

God is working,
God is working, even now.
Though we often don't know just how,
God is working even now.

Those words were the bridge over the troubled waters that flooded my brains. I could feel a praise coming my way!

• • • • •

DAY SEVEN: Thursday, September 1, 2005

The news on the television was no better than it had been on the day before. I tuned in to another channel now occupied by a familiar face. Sally Ann Roberts was a dear friend and I felt like I was looking into the face of an angel.

As she and Eric tried their best to inform those of us who were displaced and confused, I sensed their own story of unbelief. Sally gave her e-mail address and I went straight to my computer to mail her. I was glad to have some contact with New Orleans.

After breakfast, Mom called me to the phone. I could not imagine who would be calling me. It was my old friend Denise, who was a pastor at the church where our youth group had worked during the summer. She wanted to know how I was. I told her I was fine, but still trying to process this whole experience. Denise told me she had shared my address with family and friends and they would be in contact. I still could not imagine the impact this disaster would have on the whole country.

News of the disaster was broadcast over every major network. I thought about catching up on my Bible reading, but my mind was jammed with so many thoughts. I began to wonder about my friends and whether they had made it to safety. I still felt my house had escaped the high waters because it was three feet off the ground. The whole situation was so overwhelming that I'd forgotten about the words to my familiar prayer about the plight of New Orleans: *"God, one of these days you're going to wipe out New Orleans. All I ask is that you give me a warning so I can grab my purse and get out of here."* It never dawned on my mind that God was in the midst of all of this. Was this disaster an answer to a prayer, or a curse, pronounced on a city profiting from the sins of men?

I sat that entire day with my eyes glued to the grim rescue operations portrayed by the media. James called the house and told us to look outside the front door. Since Mom's house was on the corner I got a good view of the long line of school buses that were headed for New Orleans. The children would be dismissed from school on Friday so the buses could help with the evacuation. The line was over a mile long! I wanted to run to the fence and just yell "Thanks!" Finally, there was hope for the thousands stranded in New Orleans.

Those buses would drive well into the night and then on to Houston or wherever a shelter was available. My mind tossed between sad and mad, because these buses reminded me of the slave ships during the 17th century that transported people who seemed to have no say over their own destiny. Those stranded in New Orleans were "taken" to other cities and states with no knowledge of where they were going. They were promised a land over-flowing with love, shelter, and clothing, but no red beans and rice. Families were torn—apart, husbands and wives, mothers and children, brothers and sisters—landing in different shelters with no hope of ever seeing their loved ones again. That scenario was far to familiar to black people. I thought to myself *"America is doing it again."*

• • • • •

DAY EIGHT: Friday, September 2, 2005

I was up early that day, calling FEMA and the insurance company. I had left all my important papers in a plastic box on the floor of my house, so I depended on the company to recall my information. Everybody gave the same message to hold for the next available agent as I tied up Mom's phone—she did not have the call waiting feature. The news was the same wherever I called. I had to wait nearly an hour to have another agent tell me to wait again for the next agent. I could not imagine God trying to teach me patience at this stage of my life. I didn't wait nine months to be born; surely I could not wait that long on these folk to tell me what to do.

I realized that it was payday for me, so I could finally buy some clothes. I headed to the mall to discover that hurricane refugees were a given twenty percent discount on anything purchased. I hated being called a refugee or evacuee, but I loved the discount. It wasn't long before my car was loaded with packages of brand new outfits. It felt like Christmas and I was thankful that I was at home with my family. I did miss my family in New Orleans, but I prayed God would take care of them.

Now that I had some kind of ball rolling I had work to do. It would take weeks before I could return home so I had to find something to occupy my time. I called the Louisiana Baptist Convention and they had set up a command post for disaster relief. I told them that I would be happy to volunteer.

I talked with the WMU director and she was an old friend who told me not to worry. I was not worried, but concerned for the many folk who were coming to Alexandria to live in the shelter.

I headed to Sam's Club and bought lots of candy to bring to the children who would be staying at the Rapides Coliseum. All my years of training were finally going to be used. I had no time to think of myself, but what I could do for the hundreds of people about to become immediate citizens of Alexandria.

Finally, I had other thoughts in my mind besides the flooding in New Orleans. I began to communicate via e-mail to most of my friends. I had a different attitude and inner strength that came from a familiar source. My missionary skills kicked in and I was ready for duty!

● ● ● ● ● ●

DAY NINE: Saturday, September 3, 2005

I had been at Mom's for a week now and had no idea if I would ever see my Shacky Shack again. I was still holding out that my house did not get as much water as the rest of the houses, but somewhere in the back of my mind I knew the facts. The waters had finally settled, but it would take weeks to pump the water back into the river or the lake. Those taken to area shelters would never return to their old neighborhoods. Their old neighborhoods were forever changed by the flood. Even the neighborhoods that escaped the floodwaters were raided by looters as if they were shopping at the mall. President George W. Bush called in the National Guard, but none of their training had prepared them for a disaster of the magnitude that had struck New Orleans. The police were stretched beyond the limits and the stress was taking its toll. The tension was so strong that I could feel the hurt and the anger as people desperately tried to survive the worst disaster in American history.

I decided to take time for myself. I took my grandniece and her mom to lunch and to a movie. We had a great time. Being with them helped ease the stress I was trying to pretend wasn't there. I was the strong one in the family, but this situation was beyond anything I had ever faced as a missionary.

Being home for all of those days helped me to realize that Mom had been really lonely and depressed since Dad died. I remembered how much she took care of me during my two years of getting my knees replaced. I never would have made it through that time without her help. She was so glad to have me at home and even glad to be there for me during this difficult time. She had no idea what to do since I was always so independent. I noticed how much her attitude had improved since I was home. I guess she needed to be needed again. I guessed I could let her spoil me a little.

• • • • • •

DAY TEN: Sunday, September 4, 2005

For some reason, I felt the day was a new beginning on another journey of my spiritual life on this earth. All of my prayers were about to be answered in a way that I never had dreamed. God was doing a new thing that would make an impact on the nation. I was to be His vessel in helping to bring this new message to the people. I had no idea how or where, but I was willing to follow His plan.

As I got dressed, I realized how Mom was glad to have me with her at her church. Second Bethlehem Baptist Church was our family church, but most of the folks I had known had passed on. This was not the same church where I had my spiritual foundation. I knew the parents of most of the members, but they were different. Over the years I was able to accept the changes in my old church, but many of the older members had a hard time adjusting to this new church. There was a part of me that wished I could walk into the arms of Brother Waverly, Brother Eldridge, Brother Scott, and Rev. Tison. I knew I could trust them to assure me that everything was going to be alright.

I wished I could walk into the sanctuary of Franklin Avenue Baptist Church to hear our choir sing:

This is the day that the Lord has made,
I will rejoice and be glad in it.

Neither of my wishes would come true that day, however; but I knew in my heart that God was there and His words were alive and a very present help for such a time.

When I walked inside, one of the members came to hug me. She started with normal words of comfort as if I had died. Noticing my puzzled look she wanted to know why I wasn't depressed. I informed her that I was the only person in church with "everything" new on and it wasn't Christmas, Easter, or my birthday. The member was speechless. I wasn't being obnoxious. I just did not want Satan to have any part of what God was doing. She began to see me with a different attitude. She was so thankful and she promised to pray for me. I gave her a hug and told her I would be alright.

During the services the pastor prayed for the displaced persons from the hurricane. I knew these people cared, but they had no idea what to do. I decided to just keep quiet and maybe they would follow the actions of many of the other churches in the Alexandria area. Since I was not at Franklin Avenue I decided to give my tithe to Second Bethlehem. I did not mean to make a scene, but one of the members publicly announced my courage to give when I had lost everything I owned. I guess she had no idea what God was about to do. I knew that I was supposed to give my tithe matter what happened. I had grown spiritually enough to understand that everything belongs to God. Yes,

I needed a lot, but I also needed to give God what was His, and then some. I knew in my heart that God would take care of whatever I needed.

I left church that Sunday with a new hope that I ready to join in the process of healing for New Orleans. I would try to get rest because it would be a rough week. I found an old Bible in the car and I started reading a familiar passage, Job 1:21: "The Lord giveth and the Lord taketh away, blessed be the name of the Lord." I did not like reading Job or that particular verse, but I knew that I was to praise God in all things. He was up to something and I would be alright. All the verses of hope I had shared with so many popped in my head. I could feel the power of God flooding my soul. I was going to be alright. God was working just for me. I could rest in what He was planning.

GOD IS WORKING!

I MISSED MY FAVORITE CHAIR where I spent time along with God so I had to find another spot. I had been sleeping on the sofa so I could watch television all night. That was my sleeping pill. Mom had cable so I was able to enjoy Christian television, which brought many hours of strength and hope. I missed all my books and tapes, however, God was busy working that out, too.

I got the surprise of my life when I discovered extra money in my checking account. I thought I was really dreaming until I called my bank and learned the extra money had come from FEMA. What a blessing! But God was already at work as many of my friends were coming to my rescue. I prayed for wisdom to make wise decisions concerning my new finances.

I was happy to be in a place where I had no expenses, but I wanted to help Mom any way I could.

I found myself at the bank getting my accounts up to date and ordering new checks. Everybody was so kind and helpful. It took many days to get my mail, but the government had put a freeze on all our accounts. I was thankful, but I paid off all my bills. I was now debt free for the first time in a lot of years. My heart ached for the many who were stuck in unfamiliar places with no funds. I was able to get addresses from Franklin's Web site so I decided to send extra funds where needed.

I finally made my way to the command center at the Baptist building. I met Cindy and showed her my one outfit that I came to work in. I made her laugh when I told her they did not have my size at the thrift store. She told me not to worry because the WMU was going to get me some new clothes. I found a seat at the computer and went to work. I was just overwhelmed with the many calls needing help or wanting to donate. I had a ball and promised to come as often as I was needed. I met other ladies who volunteered to staff the phones. That missionary spirit was fueling my urge to move forward.

I got a recent copy of the Baptist newspaper and there was a picture of my pastor, crying as he observed the water covering our church. Seeing his picture reminded me of how much I missed him and my Franklin family. Inside the paper were pictures of the waters that destroyed many buildings on the campus of the New Orleans Seminary. Water filled my eyes as the news told the story that every church in the metropolitan area of New Orleans had been destroyed. I remembered getting calls from many desperate pastors who were left churchless and jobless.

What caught my attention in the paper was the announcement that my pastor would be preaching this Sunday at the Calvary Baptist Church in Alexandria. What a blessing! Then I wanted to cry. I had not seen or heard from Fred and Liz since the morning the hurricane hit. I could not wait to tell Mom that they were going to be in town. Fred had a weakness for Mom's t-cakes. I found Brother Brook's phone number and told him that Fred was preaching in Alexandria. That's all it took for the word to spread. My pastor was going to get the surprise of his life.

Sunday morning came and I found myself heading down the highway to surprise Liz and Fred. The big program was Sunday evening, but another one of the area pastors had asked him to preach that morning. I got to the church early and almost screamed when I saw my pastor and Liz coming down the sidewalk. I think the folks at this small country church thought several of us had lost out minds. Brother and Sister Brooks were there also. Several other members from Franklin who were living at a shelter nearby had come, too. It was like a family reunion. Of course it was sad to see Fred cry. I wished I had some of Mom's t-cakes for him.

When I told James that Fred was preaching at Calvary, he promised to go along with me. I also found Fred's Mom and his brother, who had been reported missing. God was going to do something with all of us this night! When I arrived at the church Byron, our minister of music, was there along with his family. They had evacuated somewhere in the Baton Rouge area. I was so glad to see everybody. Fred cried when he saw his mom and brother. We were all happy and sad at the same time. Again I wished I had a bag of Mom's t-cakes. It was hard and I could see the stress on Fred's face, but I knew God would get him through.

Just when we were trying to process the worst disaster in American history, Hurricane Rita showed up. She was not as severe as Katrina, but most of the western coast on Louisiana and Texas had to be evacuated. My dad's sister, Aunt Mary Lee, lived in Beaumont so she came to stay with us for a while. I was so glad to see her and she was happy to stay with us. It would take two weeks before those folks would be able to return to their homes. My aunt did not get any damage to her home, which was a blessing.

While getting settled in Alexandria, I was invited to a ladies' retreat in Michigan. I was excited to travel to my old missionary stomping grounds. I really didn't feel up to

Hurricane Katrina had destroyed my house, but not my joy. Like so many other homes along the Gulf Coast, my little "Shacky Shack" sustained a great deal of damage.

sharing with anyone, but I needed a break from hurricane war stories. This church was real special and they had been such an encouragement during my knee surgery. I was so thankful that God sent them my way. I had a new spirit as I shared with them how God's Word teaches us how to take that leap of faith. I felt like I was preaching to myself. While there, I had a chance to see my old pastor Brother Davis and his wife Mariah. They were like second parents when I had worked in Detroit. How I praised God for their love and special hugs! Mariah took me shopping, and that was so special. I think I was beginning to enjoy being pampered.

I returned home to the news that Fred was preaching in Baton Rouge and the church was having a reception for any of Franklin's members in the area. I decided that I was going to be there and James wanted to go with me. The two-hour drive was worth it when I saw familiar faces in the parking lot. The church was celebrating their anniversary and Fred was to be their speaker, but when almost 700 of us showed up it turned into a Franklin revival.

We all gathered in the parking lot and had our own praise and worship. We were all yelling and screaming like we had all won the million-dollar lottery. Once we were inside there was no stopping us. The services had to be delayed because we were crying and laughing at the same time. Cameras were flashing everywhere and everybody was trying to share their own personal story. When the service started, the Spirit moved through that place like on the Day of Pentecost. Fred was glad to see all of us and after the service he had a special meeting with us. We all sighed at the news that our church building was destroyed and our church staff displaced. My thoughts went back to that last speech I made at Franklin. Mom had a copy of the tape and I recalled the prophecy I made that we could lose everything. I had no idea God was speaking to us then, but I knew He was speaking that day. I knew He had something greater in mind for Franklin and we just had to sit and wait for His instructions. God answered my prayers concerning Franklin and at that moment I knew they were ready to become mission minded.

I had heard the news reports that perhaps by the end of October we would be allowed to return to New Orleans and start cleaning our homes. I had heard stories of mold growing so intensely that it had reached to the ceiling and thick toxic waste on the floors. I wanted to face the reality of my Shacky Shack, but there was a part of me that would rather forget about everything and just move on. But, still hoping something was saved through all the flood water, I decided to go back as soon as we were cleared to return. My big brother James would make the trip with me also. In order to even enter my neighborhood I had to have boots, gloves and a mask for the terrible odor from the rot and decay. This would not be a vacation, but rather a trip I would never forget.

NOTHING LEFT, BUT GOD

I BELIEVED THE WORDS of the old gospel hymn, "Long as I Got King Jesus, I Don't Need Nobody Else." But as my brother James and I drove through my deserted neighborhood in the Ninth Ward of New Orleans, I longed for the presence of other human beings. I longed to see the faces of the children playing in the park, or even the noise of gangsta-rap music blasting from the street corner.

The eerie silence frightened me more than the drug dealers that used to hang out in the neighborhood. Everything and everybody was gone. Not a creature was stirring, except those that you viewed under a microscope. The aroma of shrimp, po' boys, and red beans and rice had been replaced by the stench of rot and decay. This desolate place that I had called home for nearly thirty years was now a place with nothing left but God. Katrina had flushed everything away but the Lord Himself.

This place of Nothing Left But God left me overwhelmed. My stubborn, independent personality was not comfortable in this place where I was alone by fate rather than by choice. My trembling voice uttered no words of praise or thankfulness. I, too, was silent. The "whys" and "how comes" found their way to the Master's ears, but the silence remained. I gasped as James parked my car in front of what I lovingly called my Shacky Shack.

There was dried mud on the sidewalks and dead plants formed a ring around my house. On the front porch, police graffiti and my soggy welcome mat greeted me. I took my last breath of almost-fresh air and followed my brother inside. James tried to shield me from the devastation.

My beautiful house was now a mess beyond repair. *"There must be something salvageable,"* I thought before entering the place. But I was mistaken. It was as if a giant had picked up my house and shook it like a tambourine to Katrina's beat. I held on to my brother as we made our way through the black muck. My Bibles, books, and tapes were strewn across the floors in ruin.

All the material things I had held dear were gone. Still, I had to believe that in all this mess was a miracle from God. If I didn't have that hope, I surely would have lost my mind.

The only piece of furniture left standing in my little Shacky Shack was my computer desk. The top shelf held a picture of my dad and several angel figurines given to me by my kids. Through the flood of memories, I sensed God reassuring my spirit that everything would be alright.

I grabbed my dad's picture and all the angels. I found a basket to put them in. As I turned to walk away, I noticed the plastic box with all my important papers untouched by the waters. Words of praise and thanks began to flow from my heart.

My brother cautioned that we needed to get out because of the toxic waste and black mold we were breathing. I agreed, and as we reached the front door, I noticed the table with my precious African-American figurines still intact. Also on that table was the bouquet of roses made of two-dollar bills that Mom had given me for my fiftieth birthday. I grabbed the figurines and the blackened bouquet, and then took a final look at my home. I knew I'd never live there again.

Soon the men from disaster relief would come and take thirty years of my life and pile it on the sidewalk for the garbage trucks to collect. My favorite chair—where I'd spent hours studying God's Word and praying for my kids—was gone. My personal journals, which held the emotions of my heart, were gone. Everything was gone.

Touring my deserted neighborhood gave me a pain in my heart for the many who never escaped and those who would never come back. As we turned down Franklin Avenue, where my church stood, the parking lot, which had overflowed with cars on Sunday mornings, was eerily vacant. There was nothing there but the same black mold that greeted us everywhere. I saw the water line that circled our beautiful church building and water filled my eyes. It, too, was ruined. As we drove past, I realized again we had nothing left but God.

Not only was my church gone, every church in the city was damaged or destroyed by the floodwaters. Ironically, many of the bars and strip joints in the French Quarter were open for business. There was no place open to praise God, but plenty of places to drink and have a good time. I imagined Satan's laughter. Was he thinking he had finally won a battle against God's children? Then God's Spirit assured me that this battle was just beginning.

During the ride back to Alexandria, I had a lot to think about. In my heart I knew God was preaching a message to His people. Before Katrina, New Orleans was a sick city. Sin, poverty, and corruption had taken their toll on our neighborhoods, our schools, and even our churches. Now, in a sense, we had a clean slate. Perhaps God had taken all of us out of the city in order to bring a few of us back to do His work. God does not need mega-buildings to get His message out. He needs people with a mega-dose of His Spirit—people who will be obedient to His Word. He needs people who are willing to give everything so that others may come to know Jesus. I wanted to be counted among those people. Like Isaiah, my heart cried out: *"Here I am, Lord ..."* (Isaiah 6:8).

I was among the remnant of believers who would return to New Orleans with nothing but God. He took everything away so that I would have nothing left to depend upon but Him. But amid the upheaval, I made an amazing discovery: When there is nothing left but God, He is enough. He is all you need to start over again. What a foundation to build upon! God is all you need for every need. Stay close to Him, and the material concerns will take care of themselves.

I could not wait to get to my computer when I got home! I typed as fast as I could to get my thoughts just as God had revealed them to me. I went to the Baptist building and took my story to the paper, which they were glad to print. God was doing something special with my experience and I was ready.

Some of the things I found in my house had to be disinfected before I could touch them. Mom was glad to help with the washing. I was really thankful that the plastic box with my important papers was alright. Then my hands picked up my muddy birthday rose. Mom remembered how pretty it was when she had given it to me on my birthday. It was ugly and dirty from the black mold that now decorated my Shacky Shack. There had to be a message in this rose so I just put it on the top of the shelf.

THANKFULNESS

EVERYTHING I OWNED was now piled high in front of my used-to-be home. Boxes that were still packed were filled with mold and mildew, never to be opened again. There was no use in trying to dig through the foot-deep yucky mess covering the floor to look for any valuables. My good friend Becky, along with Mandy and Mike sought to differ with me, however. They donned their boots and disaster gear as if they were ready to do battle with a familiar foe. Mike led our mold safari through the junk in my Shacky Shack.

Mike discovered my Sunday hats on the top shelf of my closet and another plastic box carrying my much needed underwear. I thought to myself that God really has a sense of humor. Becky was busy busting down the door to my bedroom where she found two pillows and more angels. We did not stay long because we were afraid of breathing germs that matched the strange odors in my house. I was able to get some of the pictures off my molded walls. I said good-bye to my little Shacky Shack once again and headed back to Alexandria.

As I worked at the disaster relief center, stories poured in daily. The more stories I heard the more thankful I was. God had blessed me in spite of the storm. When I wasn't at the phones I was at the Rapides Coliseum giving candy to the children. Hundreds of people were packed like sardines with little hope of ever finding a decent place to live. I tried to listen and offer whatever advice I could. As I was blessed I was able to bless others. I received so many clothes that I was able to provide the centers with "big girl" sizes.

Through this entire experience God opened many doors for me to share my story. Folks were amazed at how calm and collected I was. I had to remind them that I was at home with my mom and that was a blessing. I never had to stand in line at the food stamp office or the Salvation Army clothing store. I was so blessed. God sent so many friends my way that I longed for nothing. Everything I needed had been supplied. I was thankful to have all my needs met, but God had a bigger blessing waiting for me.

My insurance company called and said they were going to total my house and I would get my full benefits. I was shocked since most of my friends were still fighting with their insurance companies. I was to receive a check for the full amount of my coverage. Then I remembered that voice that told me my house note would be paid off in less than three years. I was about to praise dance through Mom's house!

The day the insurance check arrived, I loaded Mom in the car and headed to Opelousas where my bank had relocated. We got to the temporary bank and within thirty minutes I had paid off a thirty year mortgage in nine months. Our God is indeed an awesome God! I was so excited I could hardly stand myself. I had no idea what I would do next, but I was a woman who was completely debt free. What a blessing! I told Mom that I was going to buy another house somewhere else. I don't think she was ready for me to leave, but I wanted another house of my own.

Kay Bennett, director of Baptist Friendship House in New Orleans, called to ask if I wanted the disaster relief team to clean out my house. Of course I would be glad for them to help. I donned my boots again and headed for New Orleans. The men came and went straight to work. It took most of the day, but I had a car filled with overlooked treasures from my house. I was so thankful to those men for all their hard work. On the way home I remembered the boxes in my attic. I called Kay and she said she would get them for me. It was a miracle that those boxes had all my pictures and Christmas decorations. There was a blessing in the storm.

Mom was surprised when I returned as if from a garage sale. I had bags and bags of stuff that needed washing and disinfecting. Mom was so glad to have something to do that she went right to work. Boris sniffed each bag and decided to sit in his bed and watch. I was like a little child at Christmas. Most of my dishes and pans were on the top shelf of the pantry so they escaped the ragging waters. I did not know if God would ever find me another house, but I had some things to get started.

God was busy at work providing another blessing. My good friends Leroy and Cecelia had decided to sell their home in Louisiana and move to Atlanta. They packed what they wanted and decided to give the rest of their furniture to me. I could hardly believe it! James and Rie went with me on my treasure hunt. By the time we loaded everything, I had enough furniture to start over again. I was so thankful for a Lay-Z-Boy recliner to replace my old recliner that I'd lost in the flood. I could not wait to christen it as my new quiet place. I secured a storage place in Alexandria, which I loaded to the brim. God was working.

I had made no decisions about my Shacky Shack in New Orleans except for the fact that I would never live in that house again. Since I was debt free I figured I was in a great position to purchase another house. I got on the Internet to begin my search for a new home. Finding a house in a safe, no flood zone in New Orleans was a bigger challenge than I could have imagined. The price of even a cheap house had risen beyond my wallet, but never out of the reach of a God who owns everything. I never worried, but I hated going through this whole house-buying process again. God was working.

I was most thankful for the many opportunities to share my story in Alexandria. Several of the schools and churches invited me to share what God had done in my life since Katrina. I did not want to share a war story to get pity or sympathy from them. I wanted to share God's blessing in the midst of the storm. One day while watching television, my eyes landed on my once-beautiful rose that was now faded and ugly with mold-stains. I tried to imagine the story this rose had buried within each ugly petal. Then the word *valuable* came to mind. It did not matter what this rose had gone through, it was still valuable. Money never loses its value. I could take this rose to any bank and each bill would be replaced with new ones. *"That's it!"* I said to myself. God gave me a message to share. It does not matter what you go through, you are still valuable. Everything God created was valuable and no matter what happens you always will be valuable. What a message—and I was ready to share it!

My good friend Cindy had invited all the minister's wives to a special retreat. I wasn't a minister's wife, but she invited me to speak, especially for those wives from New Orleans.

Seeing what took me 30 years to accumulate piled in front of my once-beautiful Shacky Shack, I truly realized that there was nothing left but God. But God was enough.

Liz flew in from Birmingham to share in the program and I was so glad to see her. I knew exactly what I was going to share. When I was introduced, I approached the podium carrying my ugly rose.

I shared my "Nothing Left but God" testimony and then drew their attention to the rose. I explained to them that Mom had given me this rose made of two-dollar bills for my birthday. It was a part of the decorations in the living room of my now-destroyed home in New Orleans. Although the rose was no longer beautiful, it was still valuable. I looked into the faces of many hurting women to tell them it did not matter what they had gone through, they were still valuable.

They may feel as ugly and stained as this rose, but their value would never change. God was moving in that place and I could feel the pain being lifted. How I praised God for my ugly rose and its beautiful message!

It was nearing Christmas and I was so blessed to be able to help so many. Most Christmases I was broke with just enough funds to buy candy for the kids and turkeys for their parents. There were many days I wished I was Santa Claus, but God always supplied whatever I needed. This Christmas was so special and God would give me a special present. I was invited to share Christmas morning with the children of one of the largest churches in Alexandria. My high school classmate was the Sunday school director so I was honored to be chosen to share my message with them.

Before I was scheduled to speak I had lunch with my good friend Becky who said she had a surprise for me. I could not imagine what it could be. Then she went to the trunk of her car and pulled out my cradle that used to hold my stuffed animals. When she and Mandy came to help clean my house they sneaked it out in a plastic bag. Mandy and Mike had it redone and it looked beautiful. I could have cried because this cradle was so special. How thankful I was for so many special friends God had sent my way.

Christmas morning I gathered my cradle and headed for the church. After I was introduced, I laid my tiny cradle in the front of the stage. I told them just how special Jesus was in my life and all that He had done for me. I had them focus on the empty cradle. It was a far cry from the manger where Jesus was born, but the significance was the same. Jesus was no longer in a manger, but in the hearts of all who would believe. I sang with all my heart the words to my favorite Christmas carol: "Sweet Little Jesus Boy." God was really working.

God had yet one more miracle before the year was over. I knew I was a gifted writer and I had a book inside, but I had no idea how to develop my gift. I had self-published several books that I'd sold at my church or at various conferences, but I knew God had something bigger for me. Just before Christmas, my niece, Nisha, encouraged me to become a member of the Christian Writer's Guild. I had never heard of this organization, but I knew their directors, Jerry Jenkins and Tim LaHaye. I fired up my computer and joined right away. I decided to attend the writer's conference along with Nisha. I never had my writings critiqued by a professional writer, but I knew it was time to go to the next level. I had the shock of my life that my niece and I had been invited to have lunch with the famous Jerry Jenkins. I also was given the opportunity to meet with some of the major editors and publishers in the country. This was an opportunity I was not ready for.

As 2005 came to an end, I was so thankful for all that God had done in spite of Katrina. My nieces, along with several relatives, made Christmas really special for me. Mom had the best Christmas ever enjoying her new recliner and color television. I did everything I could to make her life comfortable. Mom cared less about comfort, but she just hated to be alone. She was having a ball cooking for me and I was having fun eating everything.

I got another really great Christmas gift when I heard the news ever that Franklin would be having Sunday services at First Baptist Church of New Orleans. I could not wait to see everybody. I was so excited that I could hardly wait for New Year's Day. I also learned that members of Franklin living in the Houston area were meeting at Beth Moore's church. I knew God was up to something when he sent her our way. What a blessing. First Baptist Church of Houston was allowing the members of Franklin to meet on Sunday afternoons in their building. All I could do was give God praise for all He had done.

IT'S ALREADY FIXED IN 2006!

I SPENT THE WEEKEND with my good friend Deseree who now lived in Baton Rouge. We were both excited to be traveling to New Orleans to worship together as a Franklin family. The services started at 7:30 a.m. and the house was packed. Fred let me give the welcome and folks forgot they were at First Baptist and they worshipped like they were at home again. Fred announced that Istrouma Baptist Church in Baton Rouge would have a 1:00 p.m. service for the Franklinites living in the area. I immediately prayed for Fred as he traveled from service to service. I teased him that he was now what old folks called a "jack leg" preacher.

I was just too glad to see everybody. We would be having services there every first and third Sunday of every month. We had lost many members, but then I realized maybe God was up to something. It would take a people totally sold out to the lordship of Christ to ever make a difference in New Orleans. Maybe we'd had too many members. God had cleaned out every church in metropolitan New Orleans— now it was time to get busy. I believed with all my heart that Franklin was to take the lead along with First Baptist in bringing New Orleans back to the ways of God. I had to find a house soon so I could be there to help.

When I returned to Alexandria I started writing a new journal. I searched for every scripture with the word "new" in it. I made a list of every new thing God would give me in 2006. This was so exciting that I could hardly sleep. Prayer times were very special. I missed my favorite spot in my recliner, but God was here, too. Every day God was assuring me that He was working on a plan for me and I just had to wait.

I met with my bank and they qualified me for a $130,000 loan. This was because I had a credit score of 840. I had no idea what that meant, but I could not afford the monthly notes on a loan that high. I was trying to walk by faith, but those numbers frightened me. I made me another blue string and left the finding of another house up to God. I started the process of filling out papers and getting all my records in order. I really hated these games the bank played with folk, but I also knew that this is how the system works. I searched and searched, but I could not find a house in New Orleans or any of the surrounding towns.

I found another lending agency on the Internet and decided to enroll in their house buying class. I had to drive all the way to Jackson, Mississippi for the class. This agency had lots of money to loan, but the wait was too long for me. I had my doubts, but I went on with the class. While there I discovered my two senior sisters were living with a relative. I was so glad to see them and glad to know they were alright. I also met my good friend Jan who gave me more things for my new house. I just knew God was up to something.

On the fourth Sunday in January, James went with me to visit the Franklin family that met at the First Baptist of Houston. I think James was enjoying traveling watching over his little sister. The gang was so glad to see Ms. Chocolate. How I missed everyone, but I had a feeling God would do something special with this group. They were meeting every Sunday and soon they would start Sunday School. They had set up a Web site so we could keep in touch with each other. Pastor Mack was doing a great job of keeping this group together.

The most interesting stories were of the many mission opportunities the members were enjoying. One of the youth called to say how she was standing in lines to get food, water, and clothing at the very places where we used to work. One of the pastors who would never go on a mission trip was now working at a homeless shelter. He was so excited that he had learned to make a snack pack! Many of the members worked along side disaster relief workers to clean out their homes. I got so many comments how they had learned so much and could not wait to get back to work in missions. Then I remembered how I had prayed that my entire church would learn about missions. What greater teacher was there than Katrina. God was using that disaster to do great and new things.

Nisha and I traveled together to the snow-covered mountains of Colorado for the writer's conference. I was shaking in my too-tight boots as I walked into the banquet hall of the Belmount Hotel. There were hundreds of writers hoping to meet a publisher for their latest thoughts. I didn't know what to say or do, but my mind was like a sponge soaking up everything. I met with a wonderful mentor who gave me such encouragement that I headed for the computer room to compile my thoughts. When I met with the editor of a popular magazine, he was really impressed with my hurricane article. He immediately wanted to purchase my article and that left me speechless.

I came home with so much hope of achieving my goal of being a successful writer. I just had to find another place where I could concentrate. I decided to do a little house hunting on the Internet. I sent an e-mail to all my friends asking their help in finding a house. I got one response from a friend in Picayune, Mississippi. I remembered speaking at her church several times, but I never thought of living in Mississippi. She told me that she knew a realtor who just might find me a nice house in Mississippi.

Within a couple of days the realtor gave me a call with several possible houses in the Picayune area. I called my bank and got the ball rolling to secure a loan for the house. Mom took the ride with me to see the house. I met the realtor and we went to see "my" house. As soon as we turned the corner I knew this would be my next house. It was exactly what I had prayed for. It was brick, three bedrooms, air-conditioned, and had two toilets. This was a God thing—it just took a while to get it. But it was worth all the wait.

As I fell in love with my new house, my mind recalled a conversation I'd had several years ago with Liz's sister who lived in Picayune. Elaine was a member of Franklin, but I'd never spent time getting to know her. But I remembered Liz calling asking if it was alright to give my phone number to Elaine. I could not imagine what she wanted to say to me since I hardly knew her. As she and I talked on the phone, she revealed to me that during her prayer time, God wanted her to help Ms. Chocolate find a house in Picayune. I thought Elaine had lost her mind, because I just knew I would never live in Mississippi.

I did not want to be rude so I told Elaine I would come over for a visit. She had a nice house in a very white neighborhood. The house across the street was up for sale and she just knew God would provide a way for me to purchase it. I looked at the house, but decided I did not like Picayune. Located about fifty miles from New Orleans, I'd had made several trips to Picayune over the years to speak to the Roseland Park church for their ladies' tea, but I never planned to live there. I thanked Elaine for her kindness and hospitality, but I just knew God did not want me to live in Picayune.

Now, here I sat, years later, with a realtor presenting her a check for a deposit on a house in Picayune, Mississippi. *"O ye of little faith..."* I thought to myself as I drove away thanking God for my new house. It had everything I needed and then some. The neighborhood was very white and quiet. The house had just been remodeled so all I had to do was move in. I could not wait to call my bank and get the ball rolling.

My heart ached for so many that were still homeless, but I was so thankful for what God had done for me. I worked hard getting all my papers together to meet with my bank. We set a closing date for the last of March and I was excited that I would be in my new home by the first of April. I knew Satan would have to show up with his mess, but God was in control this time.

About a week before I was to go to closing the bank started acting strange. They wanted more documentation in order to process my loan. I knew something was not right, but I could not think of a reason they were so hard on me. This was the bank that had given me a loan when I had nothing and now they were giving me the runaround. I refused to get discouraged, but pulled on my blue string. Before one tear fell from my eyes God was working.

My realtor called and told me she had a banker friend in Picayune who might help me. I started thinking that God must be out of His mind to find a banker in a place where blacks had to get permission to breathe. That afternoon a strange man with a southern accent called to inform me that he would process my loan over the phone. He said anyone with a credit score as high as mine and twenty percent to put down on a house should have no problems. I almost fainted, but I knew this southern speaking man had to know my Jesus. God was definitely working and I was about to do one of those dances I had seen at the "sanctified" church. He told me to come in the day of the closing and pick up my check. What a mighty God we serve!

Friday morning, April 7, I was headed to Picayune to sign papers for my new house. I arrived at the bank to discover the person who approved my loan over the phone was the vice president. He was reading a book on how to live like a millionaire when I entered his office. I boldly told him that I was going to make him rich. We both smiled because in our hearts we both knew that God had led us to Picayune for His purposes. Terry had lived in Jackson and God miraculously opened this opportunity for him to move his family to Picayune. God had a plan for both of us and I was so thankful our paths had crossed. It did not take long to discover that Terry had a strong faith in God.

The closing went so smooth I could hardly believe it myself. The previous owner had left some furniture in the house, but I decided to spend the rest of the weekend with one of my friends in New Orleans. God had worked it out so I could get the electricity and water turned on. I would have to wait until Monday to get the gas on. I just could not believe how friendly the folks were. I had to pinch myself to see if I was dreaming.

I decided to return to my new house on Sunday evening so I would be there when the gas man came on Monday. I walked through the door of my new house and I felt like I walked into heaven. I carefully studied every nook and cranny, touching the cabinets to see if they were real. James was still afraid for me because of the many Mississippi stories we had been told as children. For some reason I was not afraid because God had already fixed everything.

Waking up hearing the birds singing their welcome to their new neighbor added to the praise flowing from my lips. I had no idea what God would do with my life in Picayune, but I was just thankful to be in a safe, clean place. Soon the friendly gas man came and I had hot water. He wanted to stay and chat, but I still had some of my New Orleans fear of strangers left inside of me. The place was as quiet as a monastery, but I enjoyed the birds and the mooing cows nearby. I felt like I had traveled back to my roots. Somebody down the street had goats and another had chickens. I had to get used to no one standing on the corner or the loud music from a night club.

When Sunday came I had no idea how long it would take to get to Franklin, so I hit the road in the dark. I had to wait in the parking lot until someone came to open the doors. Fred and Liz were glad that I had moved nearby. He shared with us that First Baptist was going to allow us to meet in their building every Sunday. What a blessing! My good friends Herbert and Becky followed me home after church to see my new house. They were so happy for me. I told them James would come next week to bring my furniture and they promised to come help unload the truck. The blessings just kept on coming! God was busy working everything out just because of His love for me.

Soon I was headed to Alexandria to get the rest of my things. I had been living out of boxes for almost eight months and I was glad to finally have a place of my own. As I busily packed my mind stayed on the many who were yet in trailers and still living out of bags and boxes. I was thankful, but prayerful that God would do the same for many others. I could not wait to share the goodness of God to those still displaced. I wanted them to know that God had the power to fix everything. What He'd done for me He would do for anyone who had the faith to believe.

James helped me load the truck and I still could not believe all the blessings of God that I was receiving. What I had lost in the storm had been replaced by an awesome God. I had more than enough, but God still was not finished blessing me. Because of Katrina I had a new and better house, new furniture, new pots, new sheets, new clothes, and best of all a new faith that could withstand any storm. God also had given me a new message of hope to a hopeless generation that was satisfied with mediocrity. I grew tired of hearing stories of survival. I wanted believers to realize that God wanted to raise us to the level of being overcomers. God was preparing me with a new message and at just the right time I would be ready.

When James and Rie got to my new house they could not believe it. Herbert and Becky were already there to help unload the truck. I was full of praise to God for all He had done for me. I had so much stuff that my house looked like a thrift store with all the boxes! James gave the house his very own inspection and advice on how to take care of the place. I missed Dad, but was so thankful to have a big brother. I think James was having a ball giving his sister orders after years of taking orders from me. He spent the rest of the day putting up my bookcases and bed. While I was admiring what little furniture I had, my good friend Jennifer called from Georgia to say they were bringing me a load of furniture someone had given to me. Now this was just too much!

Within a week Jennifer and Kelly, along with "Get Real Ministries," were parked in my driveway with two trailers of furniture. They worked all day, and when they left I thought I was looking at a picture from *Better Homes and Gardens*. It was as if Katrina had never happened. Then I realized how God was working on my behalf even through the storm. They helped me put pictures on the walls and curtains on the windows. They even gave me a washer and dryer, which I had always wanted. The place was beyond what I could ever imagine. I found a special place for my birthday rose on the coffee table that had been given to me.

I decided to take a drive around my new hometown. It was a small town, but one with a big heart. I just could not believe the friendliness of these people. I found a guy to keep my yard and he was fantastic. Everywhere I went people would go out of their way to be kind. I came home

My new home in Picayune, which I dubbed "Housey House," has been a great blessing and a symbol of how God is still in the miracle-working business.

late from church one night and ran into a police roadblock. My New Orleans attitude kicked in, but God got there first. I have no idea what they were searching for, but they sent me on my way. For the first time I felt like I was in Mayberry and the police fit the description of Sheriff Taylor and Barney Fife.

Summer came and I found a buyer for my house in New Orleans. This was a sad-glad day, but I knew I had made the right decision. I drove by for the last time and discovered that one of my senior neighbors was back in his house. I felt sorry for them, because they were in the neighborhood all alone. I promised to come by and check on them whenever I came to town.

The highlight of the summer of 2006 was the photo shoot for the magazine that had purchased my article. The editor called and asked if I would take some pictures for the magazine. I had been down this road before with Southern Baptist magazines in years past. I was very comfortable in front of the camera. The photographer met me at a food pantry near the Gulf Coast. It seemed like an all-day affair, but I was just happy to tell another side of the story. I had no sad story and I did not want any sad pictures either. Another lady who was helping with the work in the Gulfport area joined me on the pictures. When the shoot ended I was told that perhaps one of the pictures would be on the cover of the September issue of the magazine. *"God you're doing it again"* I thought.

Later that summer I was on my way to the Ridgecrest Conference Center in North Carolina for the annual Black Church Week conference. I had been a part of this event for the last ten years, but this year it would be different. All the African-American pastors from the New Orleans area had been invited. I remembered packing my rose with no idea how God would use it at the conference.

During the weeklong conference I led the early morning praise services. Before I left for the conference I had purchased a new CD by my favorite composer,

Andraé Crouch. One of his songs became the theme for the praise services:

> All because of Jesus, All because of Jesus.
> All because of Jesus we are here.
> Because of his blessings,
> All his bountiful blessings, we are here.
> We have all gathered here. We've come from far,
> We've come from near just to make a joyful
> noise unto the Lord.
> Praising God for what He's done,
> And all the victories we've already won.
> I wanna thank God that we are here.

The words were exactly what all of us needed to hear. God had opened the door for me to be an encouragement to many of the pastors.

Fred was scheduled to preach during the evening services, but I knew he was very stressed and tired. Liz was trying to keep up with him, but I could tell she was tired too. She told me that if she was asked to introduce Fred she would like me to take her place since she had her arm in a sling due to an injury. I had the shock of my life when the director of the program asked me to introduce Fred.

I knew exactly what God was going to do. I grabbed my rose and headed for the auditorium. After the special music, I approached the podium with my rose. I had no idea what I said, but I remembered looking at my pastor telling him that he was like the rose. He had been through so much that left him worn and weary, but despite all of that he was still valuable. I never heard Fred preach with such boldness and strength. It was God who was doing it again.

When I returned home I made a decision to have my house blessed on the anniversary of the storm. I was ready to celebrate the goodness of God and I wanted to share with my friends. I could feel God's Spirit moving in my new Housey House and I knew this was the place God had prepared just for me. I wanted to use the words to Andraé Crouch's song "All Because of Jesus" as the theme for the house blessing. I sent out a special invitation.

Prior to my house blessing the Baptist Association of New Orleans had invited Ann Graham Lotz, Sheila Bailey, and my favorite singer, Babbie Mason, to share in a special rally for the women of New Orleans. I could feel the hurt as I entered the building, but when Babbie sat at the piano and began to sing "God Bless America," God started working. The women rose to their feet, soaking in the presence of a God who would never leave them. They were reminded to place their faith in God, who had the power to change their circumstances.

I left the rally early because my family was coming from Alexandria to help me celebrate. Mom was glad to see I had the house clean and looking pretty. She had no idea I had help getting the place together! I could not believe

My house-warming invitation...

IT'S ALL BECAUSE OF JESUS I AM HERE...

*On August 27th last year, I said good-bye
to my newly-purchased home of nine months
in New Orleans. Two days later my home and all
my possessions were destroyed by the hurricane.
What Katrina destroyed,
God has graciously restored.*

*Because so many of you have prayed for me,
I want you to share in the blessing of my new
home. If you cannot come please send a favorite
Scripture to add to my thought jar.*

*Lots of Love,
Ms. Chocolate*

that I actually had seven people living in this house. What a blessing from God! My heart was just filled with thanks to Him for all His blessings.

Folks arrived for the house blessing and brought so much food and many more gifts. I was overjoyed. I began the celebration with my favorite song and Brother Carter offered prayer. My good friend Valerie made a suggestion that everyone in the room offer a prayer just for me as a godly woman. I was pleasantly surprised and strengthened by each prayer. I knew God was up to something and we all promised to bring this same spirit to every home restored. This was just the beginning of something great and I was so thankful.

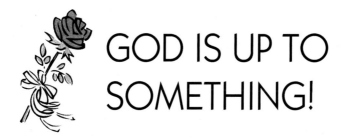

GOD IS UP TO SOMETHING!

I WAS WALKING THROUGH my house enjoying my blessings when a call came inviting me to prepare a program for a school in New Orleans. I was warned that this was a group of special education students who needed words of encouragement. I immediately picked up my rose and prayed to God for the wisdom to meet the needs of these special students. I knew these students were the rejects that only wanted to be entertained or inspired by those who had the experience of drugs, violence, gangs, or parenthood. I was inexperienced on all counts, but I yielded to God's spirit.

The day came and I purchased a beautiful red silk rose to take along with my ugly, faded, money rose. I prayed as I drove the fifty miles into a city that was still hurt and angry. Many of the children bore the Katrina experiences of their parents. There was no doubt that they had brought their frustrations with them to school with the hope that maybe someone would lend a listening ear. What they met were teachers who were just as frustrated and had no desire to listen to anyone. I knew that many of the schools were over-crowded and it would be hard to get the students' attention, or keep it for that matter. I just yielded to God and let Him talk to the students.

When I got to the school I was greeted by one of the caring staffers who was delighted that I had taken the time to share with the students. Actually, I was shaking in my crocks, but I smiled as we walked toward the library. The librarian tried to warn me about the students, and as they filed into the room, I knew she had told me the truth. I could see pain and "What's up with this?" written all over their faces. I would always get the children to yell my favorite f-word: "FANTASTIC," but they preferred some of the f-words from the 'hood.

I sat down in front of them and shared my flying story and that got their attention. I brought out my ugly rose and told them how I found it on the floor of my flooded house in the Ninth Ward. They noticed right away that it was made from money. Their hungry eyes ate my every word. Then I brought out the beautiful red silk rose which they totally ignored. When I asked them which rose they preferred,

The rose that Hurricane Katrina could not destroy has traveled with me to many places and has served as a symbol of encouragement to many.

they all wanted the money rose. When I asked why, they all replied, "Ms. Chocolate, that's money!"

I looked right in their eyes as I drew them into my Katrina experience. "Many of us, like this rose, have been through a lot that left us feeling as ugly and crumbled as this rose, but it never lost its value. We are as valuable as this rose because we were created to be great, to be successful, to be a leader, and to be fantastic. Nothing we can ever experience will change our value." I wished I was in church because I felt a sermon coming! I had their attention and they wanted to know if they could have the ugly rose. I challenged them to continue onward and upward to become the fantastic persons they were created to be.

As I left the school, I knew God was up to something and I was ready. I knew in my heart that God was just getting started with this rose. I had the opportunity to attend a woman's conference to share my Katrina experience. I knew those ladies expected tears and a war story, but they got the surprise of their lives. I walked my happy, contented self to the conference with my birthday

I was excited to have my story published and to appear on the cover of a magazine.

rose in tow. They had no idea what I was going to say, but when I finished they were the ones doing the crying. So many of them had gone through hell in the two years since the storm and their self-worth had been beaten down by the fierce winds of deception and depression. I felt release and relief on their faces as God moved through the rose. They saw beyond its ugliness and grasped its value. The ladies encouraged me to write a book about my rose.

When the magazine hit the stands, my picture was right in the middle of the cover. That added a few inches to my already inflated ego but I just gave God praise for what He was doing. I was more impressed that I was referred to as a Katrina hero and not a survivor. I did not simply survive Katrina, I overcame Katrina. God took me to a higher level that even I could have imagined. He was up to something and I just wanted to be in the midst of what He was planning. Within the covers of the magazine were several pictures of my flooded house and my birthday rose. God was using me to tell His story all over again.

I took those ladies' advice and had my story published. It is my prayer that as you have read my story that you are strengthened and encouraged.

# EPILOGUE

EARLY IN 2007, my pastor called and asked me to direct the missions ministry at Franklin Avenue Baptist Church. I knew God was up to something. This is a job I love and cannot wait to see what God will do. The people are ready for missions now that they have tasted it for themselves. There are now eight mission teams in place and God is doing a marvelous work in their lives. All of my fussing and praying these last few years are coming to fruition and I just give God all the praise and honor.

During the summer we started having a community service under a tent on our parking lot. As the contractors work on our building, God's church is still at work. Our Katrina experience is a constant reminder to us that church is not about a building; it is about a people telling the story of Jesus. It's about people meeting the needs of others. We furnish food to over 400 families in the community, and that's another blessing. The men have formed a missions team that gives free lawn care to those in Habitat homes. All I can say is "Praise God!"

Each day I am blessed by memories from the storm. When the anniversary of the storm comes around again, I likely will find myself crying and reliving the journey from New Orleans to Picayune. I will join the hundreds who will fill churches and schools, sharing stories and prayers. Our hearts will unite, remembering the lives that were lost and the devastation that remains throughout the city. We will remember those who will never return as well as those who returned to nothing.

Even so, among the sad stories are voices filled with praise to God for the many miracles He brought forth as a result of the storm. I am thankful to be one of those miracles.

To order additional copies of *The Birthday Rose*, write:

Gwen "Ms. Chocolate" Williams
136 Veronica Drive
Picayune, Mississippi 39466
(601) 798-3548
E-mail: CHOCOLATELAVERN@aol.com

OTHER RESOURCES BY MS. CHOCOLATE:

MUSIC

Old Fashion Singing and Story-telling
A CD featuring stories of laughter and faith mixed with favorite hymns.

BOOKS

Speak Lord, for Thy Servant Is Listening
A prayer journal for spending forty days in silence with God.

A New Look at Prayer
A book that looks at what happens when God does not answer our prayers. What happens when He makes us wait too long?

Journey into One
Learning to become intimate with God.

Fred's Faith
A book that helps children learn how to develop their own faith in God.

The Prayer of Jabez
A wonderful and touching story to encourage the hearts of children everywhere.